Build a grow tower

BY Stan Secretan

Thanks to the universe for making living things possible.

Table of contents

PROLOG

This is the story of the start of hydroponic fun leading to the design for the Grow tower plans.

I saw several hydroponic displays at the garden show in Boise a couple years ago. I was intrigued with the simplicity of hydroponic systems.

By total coincidence I was at Lowes Home Improvement store the next day and they had a rack full of large discontinued PVC pipe fittings. They were very dirty from storage, and they were all 6 inches. The prices were marked down from over ten dollars to 50 cents and under. Well obviously they just wanted to get rid of them.

Thinking about the hydroponics exhibits I had seen the day before I thought I could build a grow tower from all of these 6 inch pipe fittings.

I bought all of them. About ten each of several type "T" fittings and couplings.

A few days went by as I thought about what to do. I started to look at hydroponics on You Tube. Wow! There are hundreds of designs and ideas. Some are great, and many not so great. It didn't take me long to decide on a plan of how to use my box of fittings.

Chapter 1

The prototype

Well, so there I was. A plan in mind and a few sketches.

I started to build my first hydroponic tower.

The idea is to have pockets that hold your seedlings that fertilized water can drizzle over the roots. The water is then recycled from a catch basin. A submerged pump attached to a pipe lifts the water up to again rain down on the roots.

I decided on twenty pockets distributed evenly around the length of a six inch diameter tube. The tube on the first model was made up of all the "T" fittings glued together making a six foot tall structure. It took a little creative plumbing to make all twenty pockets to hold the seedlings yet allowing the water to run free into the collection basin.

The assembly looked pretty good all white plastic but stood out a little too much so I painted it green with an enamel spray can.

Figure page 23 shows tower center structure after a summer season of growing.

I bought a two foot diameter resin basin from Lowes and mounted the tube assembly in the basin using four small turn buckles too center the pot tube in the basin.

I bought 3 items on line. A pump. The pump has to lift the water over six feet high.

A Timer. The timer can be set for fifteen minutes on and fifteen minutes off continuously. The third item, maybe the most important, is the plant nutrient. I bought enough nutrient from www.towergarden.com for a season of growing.

The amazing thing is how much the plants drink as they get big. Especially the tomatoes.

Keeping the basin full of nutrient flavored tap water is essential. Your plants will wilt almost instantly if the pump runs dry as well as the pump will break down if run dry.

I installed the pump on the floor of the resin basin with a hose going up to the top of the unit terminating through a cover. The power cord exited through a hole drilled in the upper ridge of the resin basin. The resin basin was good, since you can drill holes in contrast to a maybe nicer ceramic basin that can't be readily drilled.

I filled the basin with tap water and a cup of tower garden "A" nutrient and a cup of "B" nutrient. I then plugged the pump into the fifteen minute timer outlet, which I had hung away from rain and sprinklers. It was plugged it into a GFIC out door safety plug on the patio.

I could see the water flow over the perforated drain cover and drip down into the 6 inch tube onto the 20 tapered green drain cones installed inside each of the twenty grow locations.

Planting the prototype

I was ready to plant and watch it grow. My confidence was pretty low on a scale of one to ten. Maybe a five at best. Starting from seed was unappealing, too slow and delicate. Lowes had a huge assortment of starter plants for a buck or so a piece. I bought twenty of an assortment of all types of baby plants. Kale, Peppers, Tomatoes, Broccoli, Geranium, Lettuce.

I brought these all home; outside with the garden hose gently washed all the soil away from the roots of each one leaving a tangle of white roots dangling from the very young plants.

Within minutes I had stuffed the roots of each plant into one of the twenty grow locations on the grow tower. I now had twenty plants ready to grow big and get healthy.

It seemed to be a pretty drastic method of planting. The poor plants look so stripped after I had washed the soil off. The water was running from the pump and dripping nicely onto the roots for fifteen minutes and then draining for fifteen minutes and so on from the first day on.

Every day I looked, ready to replace dead entrants to my hydroponic garden. Day one all looked good,

Day two still ok. Day three all the plants were alive and some obviously were growing bigger.

Amazing! None died! Honestly, they all lived and were rushing to take over the grow tube until it disappeared.

Kale and broccoli grew best with peppers a close second until the tomatoes took over. Geraniums grew easily from shoots placed later in a vacant pot near the bottom of the tower.

What fun. I was totally overwhelmed. I didn't dream such a success was possible.

Washing off the roots getting ready to plant in the tower. I didn't want to get too much dirt in the water basin as it might clog the pump.

The first week after planting

2 months later. Amazing!

Kale gone wild

Tomatoes looking pretty good

First pepper

18

After 4 months the tomato plant on the bottom has taken over the tower. I should have started to trim it but it was to much fun to watch it take over.

Roots from a season's growth

The tower after the season

Chapter 2

Let's build a tower

The design goals

Make the assembly fun, good looking, low cost and easy to build requiring few tools.

Provide enough grow tubes to provide variety but manageable.

Provide a water basin to store at least a week of water mixed with nutrient. Water loss from evaporation and plant growth require constant replenishing of the water and nutrient.

A pump is needed to circulate the water/nutrient.

Provide a basin to collect the water/nutrient.

A timer to control the pump is needed. Stop and go is better for the root growth and reduces fungus growth from excessive wetting.

4 foot grow tower assembly GT100

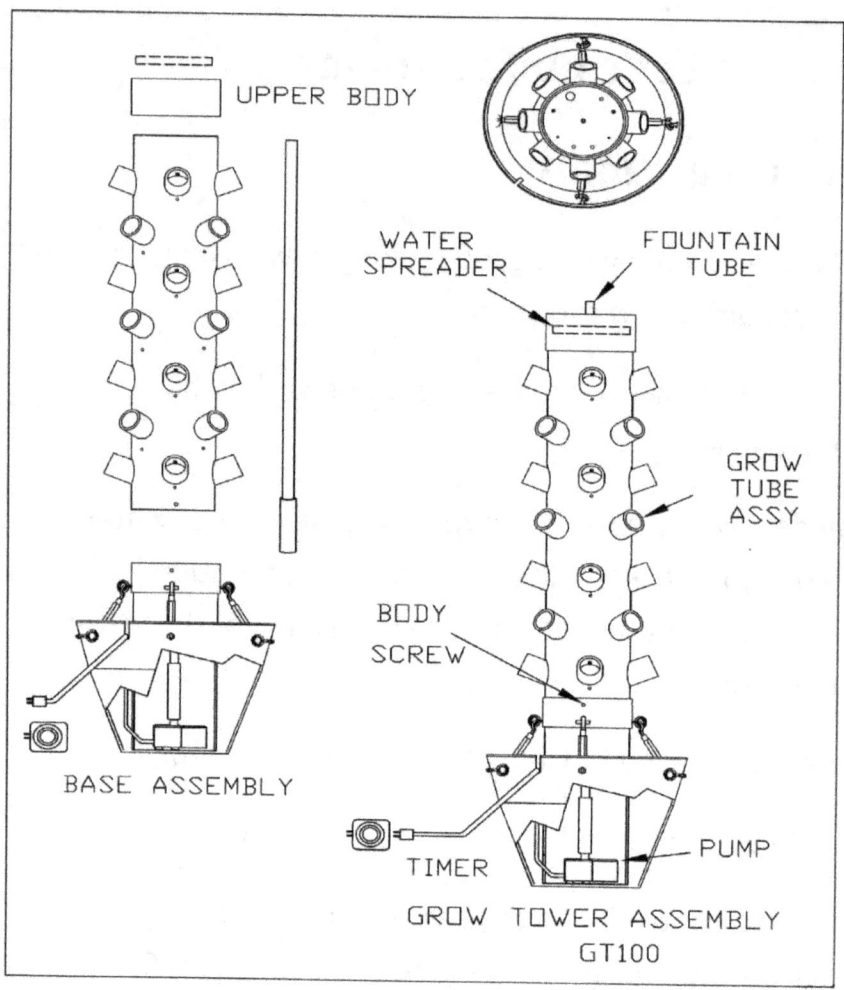

UPPER BODY

WATER SPREADER

FOUNTAIN TUBE

GROW TUBE ASSY

BODY SCREW

BASE ASSEMBLY

PUMP

TIMER

GROW TOWER ASSEMBLY
GT100

The tower is detailed in two sizes. 4 foot tall with 28 grow tubes and 3 foot with 20 grow tubes to plant seedlings in.

3 foot grow tower assembly GTS100

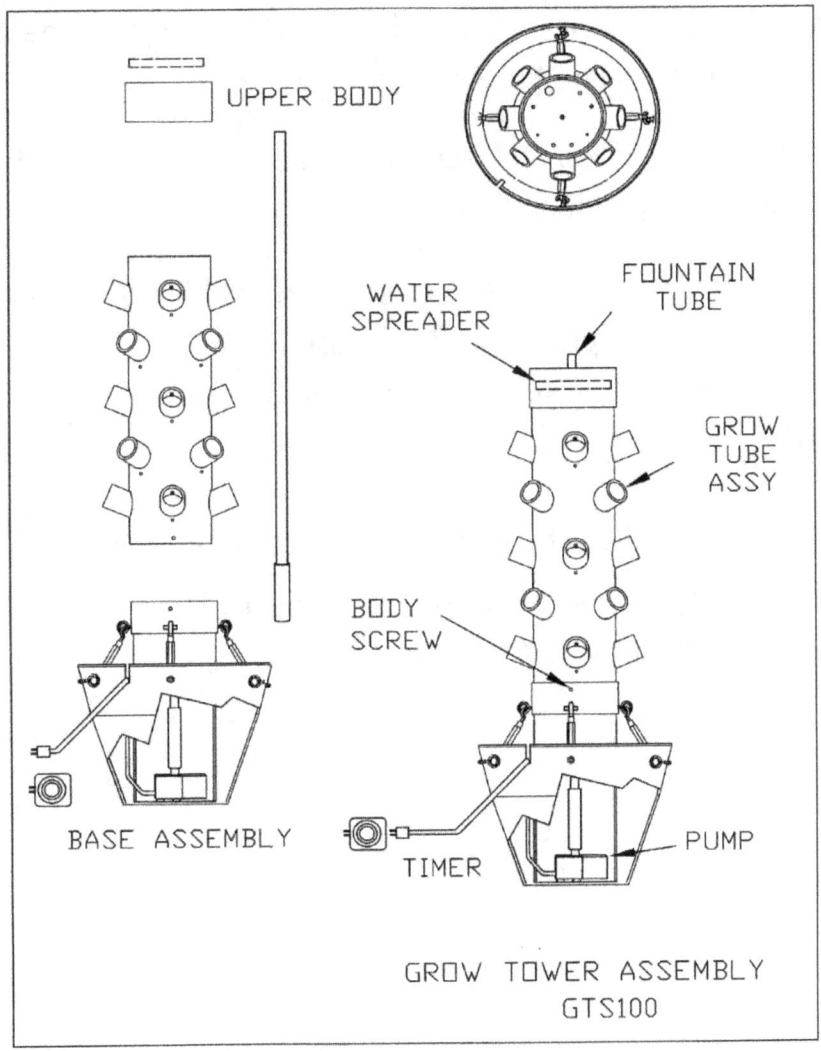

UPPER BODY

WATER SPREADER

FOUNTAIN TUBE

GROW TUBE ASSY

BODY SCREW

BASE ASSEMBLY

TIMER

PUMP

GROW TOWER ASSEMBLY
GTS100

The design is the same for both using almost all the same parts. GT part number prefix is for all the 4 foot model parts and GTS prefix is for parts that are different from the GT parts when making the 3 foot smaller model.

The tower is 2 main sections. The base assembly and the grow tube assembly.

The base assembly is a complete assembly ready for installation of the upper grow tube assembly. The two sections provide an easy disassembly point for pump access.

First: Let's look at the finished product after a month of growth in May. In the sun during the day and in the garage at night to avoid the frost

4 foot and 3 foot tower

Select a tower size

To start, decide on the size Grow Tower you want.

Select a basin about 16 inches tall for the 4 foot tower or 14 inches for a 3 foot tower. A resin basin is best. It's light weight and easy to drill and does not have a drain hole in the bottom about $16 for the smaller and $20 for the larger basin.

 After deciding on the size, be sure to get a basin that won't leak. Some very cheap molded square basins tend to crack on the bottom. The resin ones are pretty good and very attractive. You can use a larger basin for either model. And even a 24 inch diameter for the 4 foot by making the support tube a couple inches taller. The turnbuckles will still work if extended.

Note: Get the basin before cutting your support tube GT102 or GTS102 to length.

First a few words about the 6 inch pipe options.

There are two main pipe options.

1) A thin wall, white pipe with 1/10 inch wall thickness. Plenty strong for the tower and very easy to work with. You can order a 54 inch long pipe from www.McMasterCarr.com   Part # 2426K27 Enough to make one 3 foot tower or one 4 foot tower.

2) A thick wall .20 (direct burial sewer pipe) is a very pretty green color. It costs about $36 for a ten foot length. Enough to make both a 3 foot and a 4 foot model or two 4 foot models.

The same material is available in a 2 foot length drain pipe at Lowes about $16 each. Long enough for the 3 foot tower but not the 4 foot tower. You will need two of the 2 foot lengths to build a 3 foot tower. One for the main tube GTS101 and another for the support tube GTS102.

Lowes or Home Depot will cut the ten foot pipe to fit in your car if you ask.

Check in your town under plumbing supplies for other vendors to get the 6 inch PVC pipe in order to get the best price.

Make the following decisions after reading through the "Build a Grow Tower".

1. Build a 4 foot tower with 28 grow tubes or a 3 foot tower with 20 grow tubes. The 3 foot is quite a bit smaller and can be placed on a bench or small table for easy access.

2. Use the thin wall or thick wall tube. The green thick wall is very nice looking. The pipe is heavier to handle and drilling the 2 inch holes a bit harder but very doable. Cost is about the same in the end maybe a little more for the green tube.

   Easiest is the 54 inch thin wall pipe delivered to your home in a few days from McMasterCarr.com. $19+ shipping. You can also order the tube GT107 and the coupling to make GT 103 and GT104 at the same time from Mc Master.

See the parts list chapter 8 for part numbers and a complete parts list for both models.

Fabricated parts for the 4 foot tower

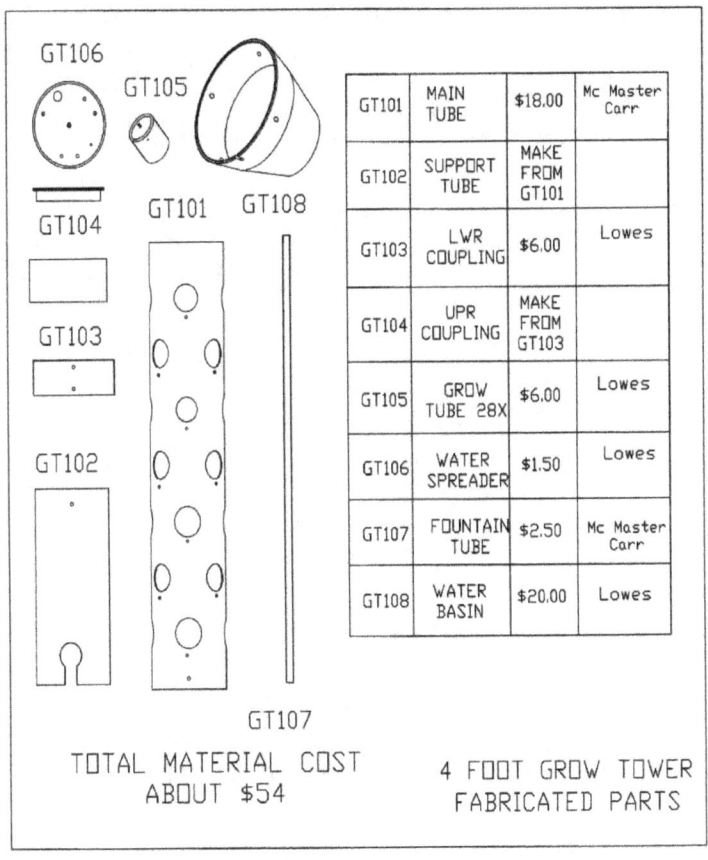

GT101	MAIN TUBE	$18.00	Mc Master Carr
GT102	SUPPORT TUBE	MAKE FROM GT101	
GT103	LWR COUPLING	$6.00	Lowes
GT104	UPR COUPLING	MAKE FROM GT103	
GT105	GROW TUBE 28X	$6.00	Lowes
GT106	WATER SPREADER	$1.50	Lowes
GT107	FOUNTAIN TUBE	$2.50	Mc Master Carr
GT108	WATER BASIN	$20.00	Lowes

TOTAL MATERIAL COST
ABOUT $54

4 FOOT GROW TOWER
FABRICATED PARTS

Fabricated parts for the 3 foot tower

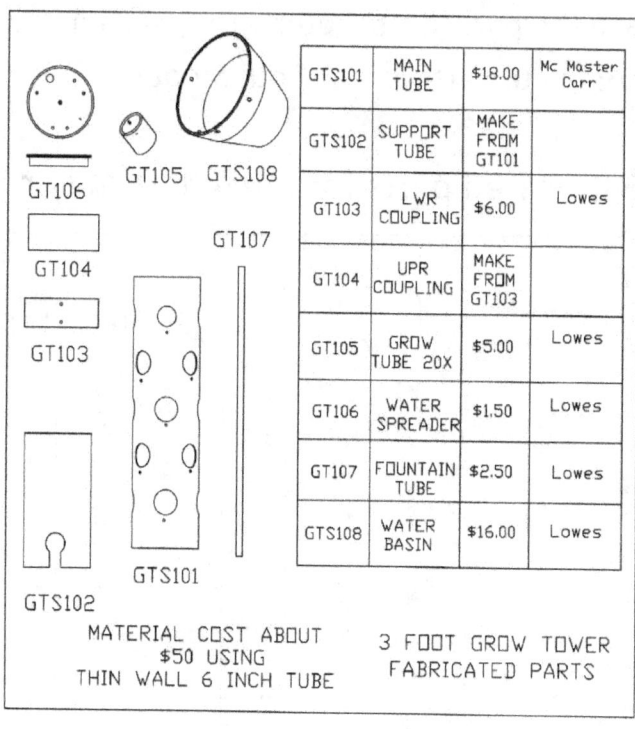

GTS101	MAIN TUBE	$18.00	Mc Master Carr
GTS102	SUPPORT TUBE	MAKE FROM GT101	
GT103	LWR COUPLING	$6.00	Lowes
GT104	UPR COUPLING	MAKE FROM GT103	
GT105	GROW TUBE 20X	$5.00	Lowes
GT106	WATER SPREADER	$1.50	Lowes
GT107	FOUNTAIN TUBE	$2.50	Lowes
GTS108	WATER BASIN	$16.00	Lowes

MATERIAL COST ABOUT $50 USING THIN WALL 6 INCH TUBE

3 FOOT GROW TOWER FABRICATED PARTS

Chapter 3

Making the base parts for a 4 foot tower

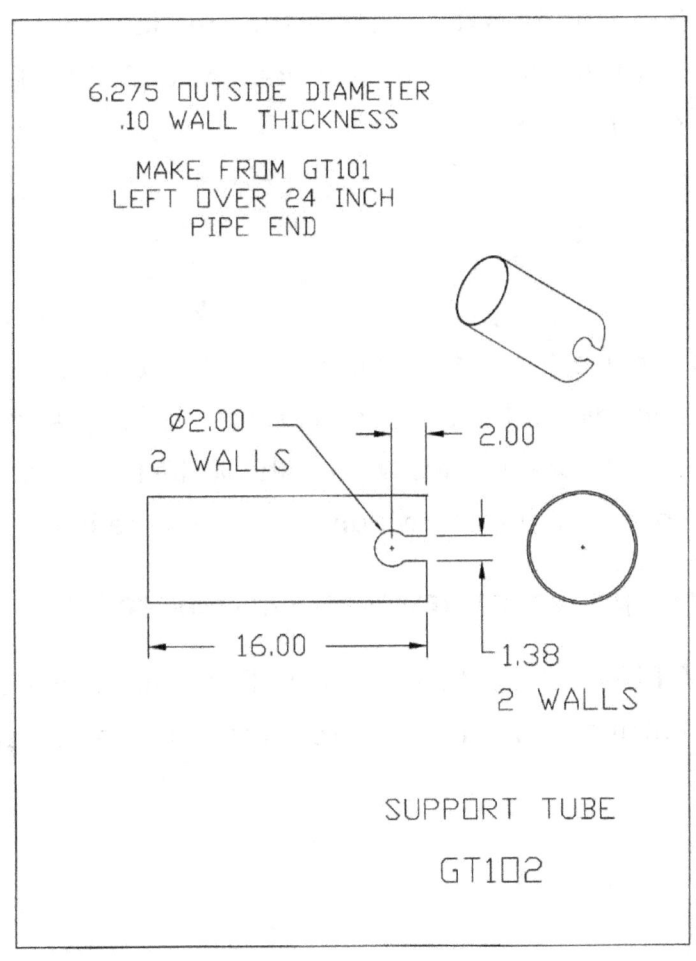

6.275 OUTSIDE DIAMETER
.10 WALL THICKNESS

MAKE FROM GT101
LEFT OVER 24 INCH
PIPE END

Ø2.00
2 WALLS

2.00

16.00

1.38
2 WALLS

SUPPORT TUBE

GT102

4 foot support tube

Drawing GT102 details the Support tube made from 6 inch PVC tube for the 4 foot tower and Drawing GTS102 is for the smaller 3 foot tower

I found it is easiest to cut the large diameter tube length using a table saw with a tungsten carbide blade up about 1 inch. Make the cut by rotating the tube while held against the fence or a wall the correct distance from the blade.

Please wear protective glasses as chips tend to fly.

Drawing GT103 details the lower coupling. The coupling is made by cutting a 2 inch length from the end of a standard

6 inch white PVC pipe coupling.

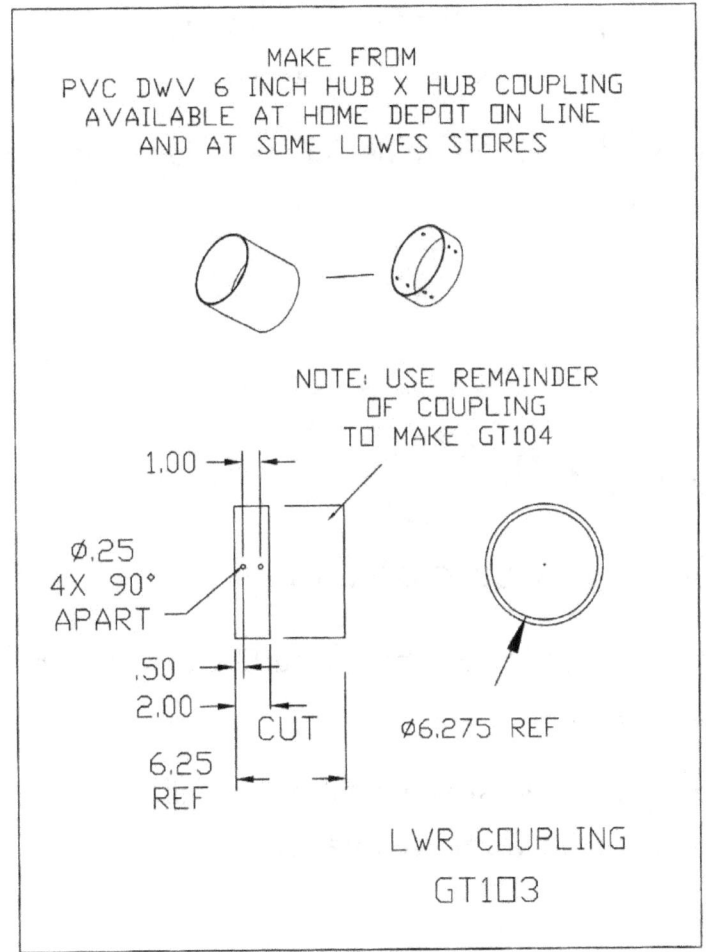

MAKE FROM
PVC DWV 6 INCH HUB X HUB COUPLING
AVAILABLE AT HOME DEPOT ON LINE
AND AT SOME LOWES STORES

NOTE: USE REMAINDER
OF COUPLING
TO MAKE GT104

1.00

Ø.25
4X 90°
APART

.50
2.00

CUT

Ø6.275 REF

6.25
REF

LWR COUPLING
GT103

Save the rest of the coupling for making the upper coupling GT104.

Locating the 4 holes in the coupling is easy if you take a piece of masking tape and wrap it around the tube overlapping then cutting. Remove the tape and measure length and divide by 4. Mark the tape and return to the coupling. Drill at the marks now 90 degrees apart.

Use a small pocket knife blade to de bur the inside ends of the coupling pipe.

Chapter 4

The 4 foot tower base assembly

Decide and purchase your basin before cutting the support tube GT102 to length.

If you are in a hot weather area a larger basin will require less attention to refilling from evaporation.

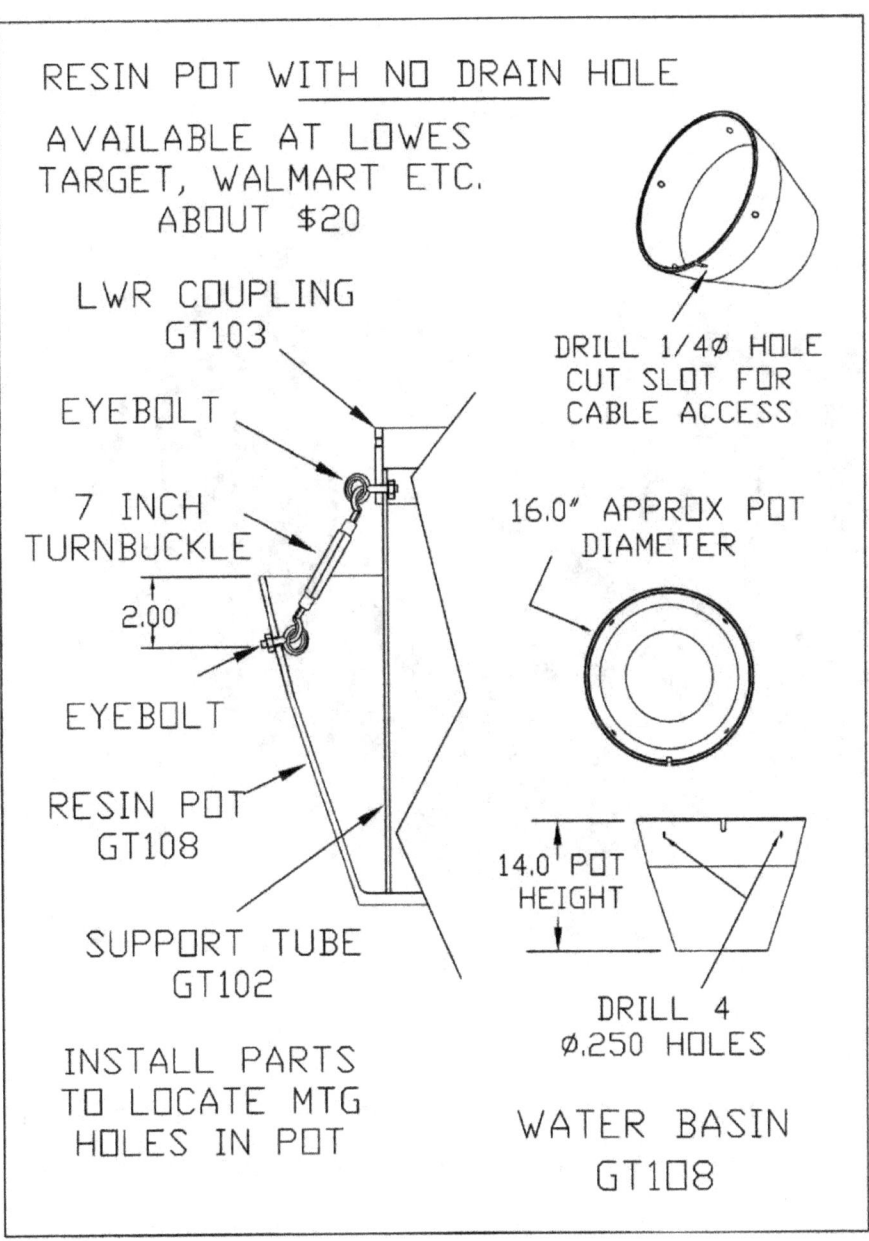

RESIN POT WITH NO DRAIN HOLE

AVAILABLE AT LOWES
TARGET, WALMART ETC.
ABOUT $20

LWR COUPLING
GT103

EYEBOLT

7 INCH
TURNBUCKLE

2.00

EYEBOLT

RESIN POT
GT108

SUPPORT TUBE
GT102

INSTALL PARTS
TO LOCATE MTG
HOLES IN POT

DRILL 1/4∅ HOLE
CUT SLOT FOR
CABLE ACCESS

16.0" APPROX POT
DIAMETER

14.0' POT
HEIGHT

DRILL 4
∅.250 HOLES

WATER BASIN
GT108

Drill 4 holes 1/4 inch diameter down 2 inches from the rim using the tape method to locate 90 degrees apart Install 4 eyebolts.

Temporarily install 4 eyebolts in the GT103 coupling.

Now install 4 turnbuckles with length all about the same leaving about 1/2 inch to tighten. Measure the distance from the coupling midpoint to the basin floor. It will be about 16 inches for the 4 foot tower to the midpoint of the coupling depending on the exact height of your basin.

Cut the length of the support tube CT102 to 16 inches more or less depending how your basin size affects it.

Slide the GT 103 coupling over the finished GT102 support tube 1 inch and drill 4 holes through the support tube using the GT103 as a guide. Install 4 eye bolts and tighten.

Locate the cable slot somewhere on the rim of the basin. Drill a 1/4 inch hole down about 1 inch from the rim. Hack saw or sabre saw down slotting the hole to be a snug fit to the pump cable.

Place the pump on the floor of the basin inside the Support Tube. The pump, (see parts list chapter 8) has suction cups holding it to the floor of the basin and is located inside the support tube.

The completed base assembly is light weight and easy to handle. When filled with water/nutrient it becomes very stable.

Chapter 5

The 3 foot tower base assembly

Pretty much the same as the 4 foot assembly but with a smaller basin

Decide and purchase your basin before cutting the support tube GTS102 to length.

Again If you are in a hot weather area a larger basin will require less attention refilling from evaporation.

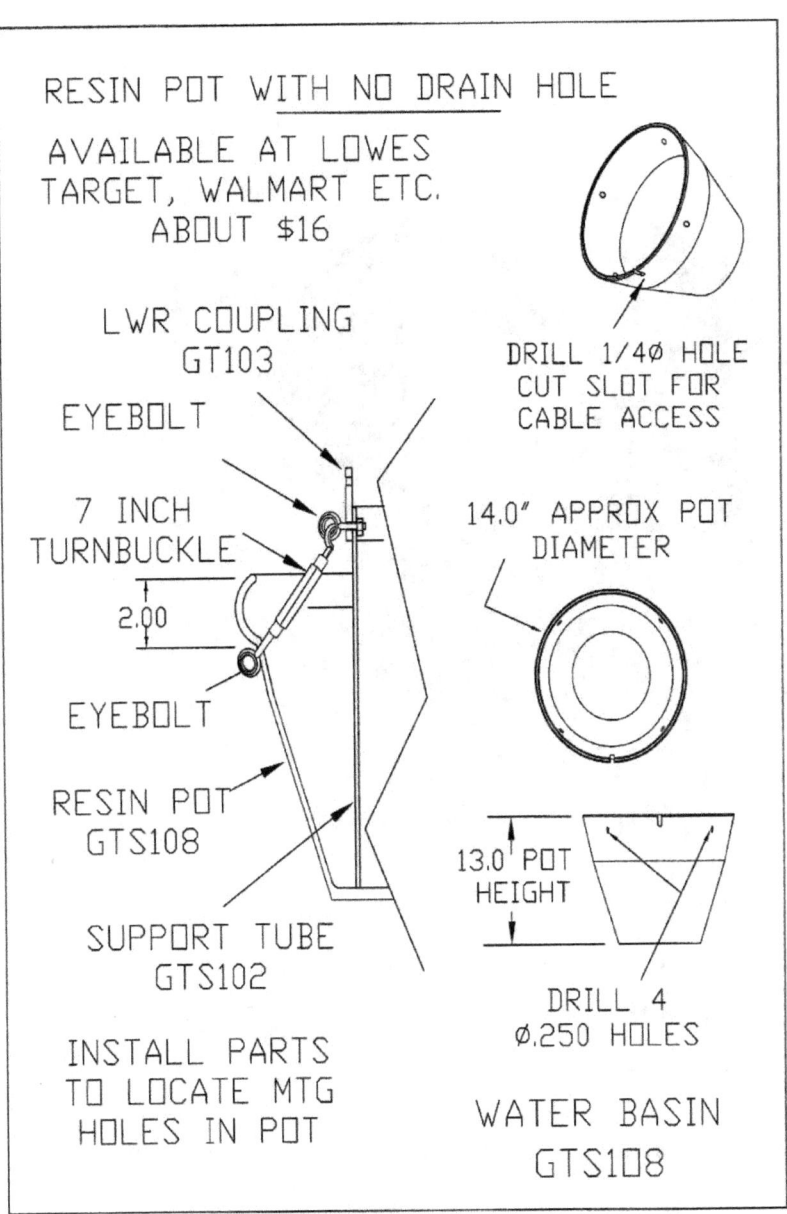

RESIN POT WITH NO DRAIN HOLE

AVAILABLE AT LOWES
TARGET, WALMART ETC.
ABOUT $16

LWR COUPLING
GT103

EYEBOLT

7 INCH
TURNBUCKLE

2.00

EYEBOLT

RESIN POT
GTS108

SUPPORT TUBE
GTS102

INSTALL PARTS
TO LOCATE MTG
HOLES IN POT

DRILL 1/4Ø HOLE
CUT SLOT FOR
CABLE ACCESS

14.0" APPROX POT
DIAMETER

13.0 POT
HEIGHT

DRILL 4
Ø.250 HOLES

WATER BASIN
GTS108

Drill 4 holes 1/4 inch diameter down 2 inches from the basin rim using the tape method to locate 90 degrees apart Install 4 eyebolts.

Temporarily install 4 eyebolts in the GT103 coupling.

Now install 4 turnbuckles unscrew the right hand thread end and scrap the hook end. Use a eyebolt screwed in thru the basin into the turn buckle. Leaving about 1/2 inch or more to tighten. Measure the distance from the coupling midpoint to the basin floor. It will be about 14 inches for the 3 foot tower to the midpoint of the coupling depending on the exact height of your basin.

Cut the length of the support tube CT102 to 13 inches more or less depending how your basin height affects it.

Slide the GT 103 coupling over the GTS102 support tube 1 inch and drill 4 holes through the support tube using the GT103 as a guide. Install 4 eye bolts and tighten.

Locate the cable slot somewhere on the rim of the basin. Drill a 1/4 inch hole down about 1 inch from the rim. Hack saw or sabre saw down slotting the hole.

Place the pump on the floor of the basin inside the Support Tube. The pump has suction cups holding it to the floor of the basin and is located inside the support tube.

The completed base assembly is light weight and easy to handle. When filled with water/nutrient, it becomes very stable.

Chapter 6

Making the upper assembly

The upper assembly is actually several parts. The main tube with grow tubes attached, the upper coupling GT103, The upper coupling GT104, the water spreader GT106, the water fountain pipe GT107 and a short piece of 1/2 inch clear hose to connect the pump to the fountain pipe.

Building the main tube takes a little while but the beauty of this project is that all the parts are very forgiving. A misplaced hole or slip when measuring is easily forgiven. Scrap the part it's cheap, or just go with it, nobody will notice or care.

The main tube assembly has 28 grow tubes for the tall tower and 20 for the small tower. Each grow tube has a sheet metal screw holding it in place at a slight angle to the main tube. You should use a stainless steel screw. #6 - 1-1/4 inch long.

Available from Mc Master Carr part # 90198a182 about $7 for a pack of 50

I sealed the remaining crack and the screw head with DAP Dynaflex 230 clear sealant locking the tubes in place as well as to stop leaking outside the main tube. The sealant, available at Lowes and Home Depot, is easy to squirt on and with a finger wipe excess away. It is white at first and dries clear.

By sealing each grow tube to the main tube you can then place the tower on a deck, and the floor and surrounding area will remain dry.

The grow tube mounting screw is extra-long and protrudes into the grow tube making it easy to install and provides a resting place for the roots to grow around holding the growing plant in place.

See detail GT101 or GTS101 to make the Main Tube. Either wall thickness PVC 6 inch tube can be used. Drilling 2 inch holes in the thick wall is a little harder but still pretty easy with a new 2 inch hole saw. If you have a drill press us that but a hand drill motor will work just as well.

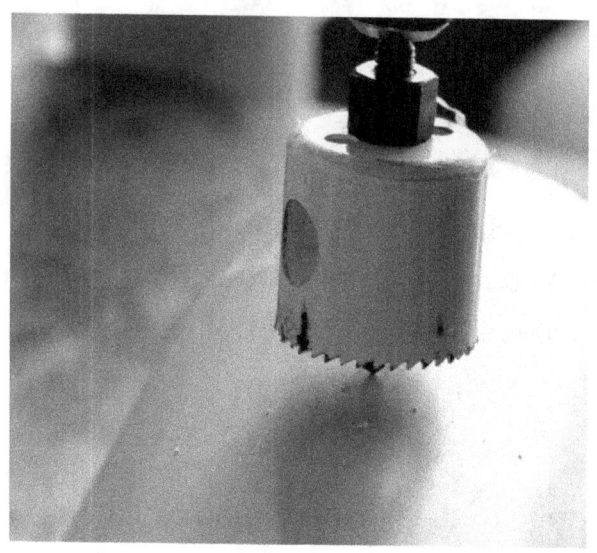

I found that cutting the main tube was easiest on my table saw. With the blade up just a half inch or so and aligning the long stock tube against a wall with the blade at the right cutting distance I could then rotate the tube around until the cut was finished.

To locate the grow tube holes in the Main Tube and getting spacing right I bought two 4 foot lengths of flat aluminum 1/8 thick by 1 inch wide and located on one the 3 hole pattern drilling 1/4 inch holes and 3/16 inch holes at each grow tube location with the template flush with the end of the 6 inch Main Tube. I made two templets so as to not confuse the 3 hole with the 4 hole spacing.

I could then place the templates on the 6 inch tube and drill the 3/16 screw holes and 1/4 inch holes for locating the 2 inch hole pilot drill. I put an extra hole in the end of the templet to locate it from markings on the 6 inch tube locating the hole patterns every 45 degrees around the tube.

To locate the 45 degree intervals I placed masking tape around the 6 inch tube overlapping and cutting it to the exact circumference of the tube. I then removed the tape and divided its length by 8 and marked 8 locations.

Placing the tape back on the tube, I now had 45 degree locations around the tube.

It was then easy to place one template for every other of the 8 locations around the tube. The same with the other template.

I then opened up the 1/4 inch holes using a 2 inch hole saw with a 1/4 inch pilot drill to drill the 20 or 28 2 inch holes.

A 2 inch hole saw is available at Lowes or Home Depot, About $20. Please make the templates to locate the 2 inch and 1/4 inch diameter holes for either the 3 foot or 4 foot model. It's so easy to make a mistake without the template.

Drilling the main tube using a template.

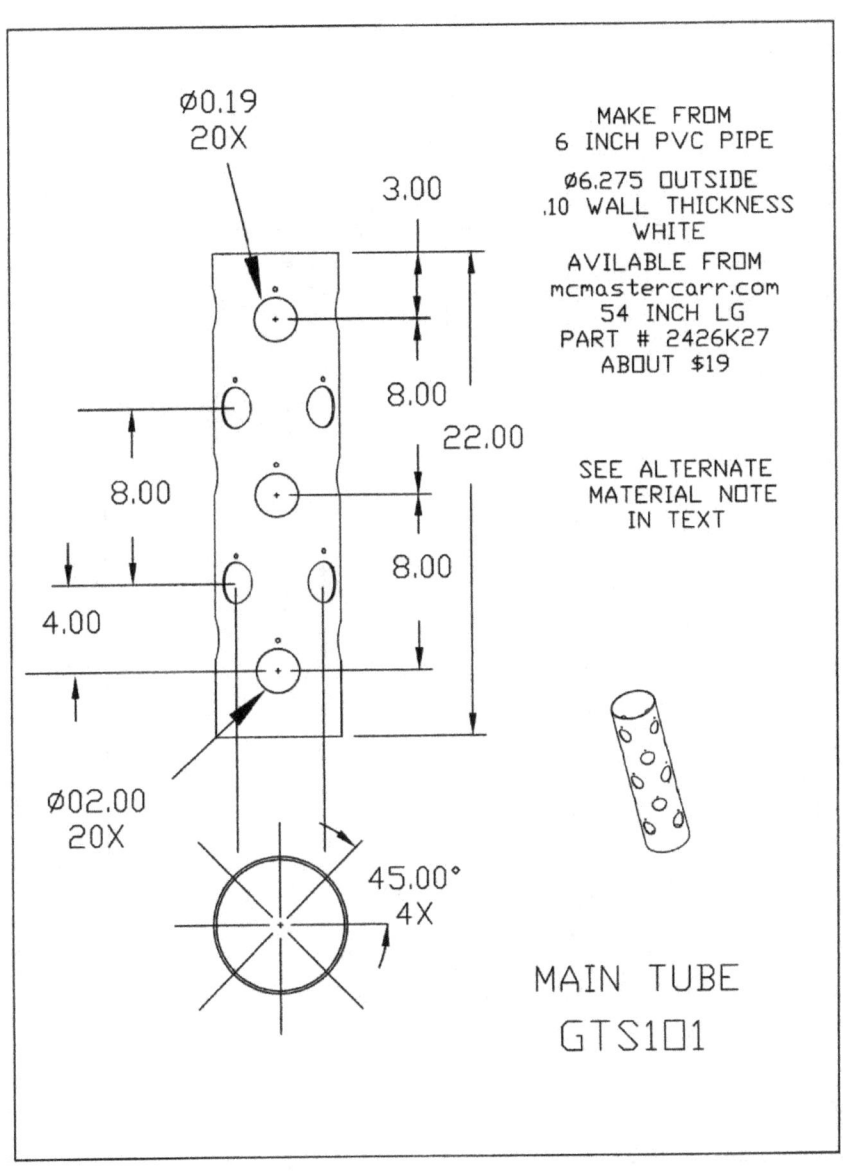

Ø0.19
20X

3.00

MAKE FROM
6 INCH PVC PIPE

Ø6.275 OUTSIDE
.10 WALL THICKNESS
WHITE

AVILABLE FROM
mcmastercarr.com
54 INCH LG
PART # 2426K27
ABOUT $19

8.00

22.00

SEE ALTERNATE
MATERIAL NOTE
IN TEXT

8.00

8.00

4.00

Ø02.00
20X

45.00°
4X

MAIN TUBE
GTS101

Main tube 3 foot tower

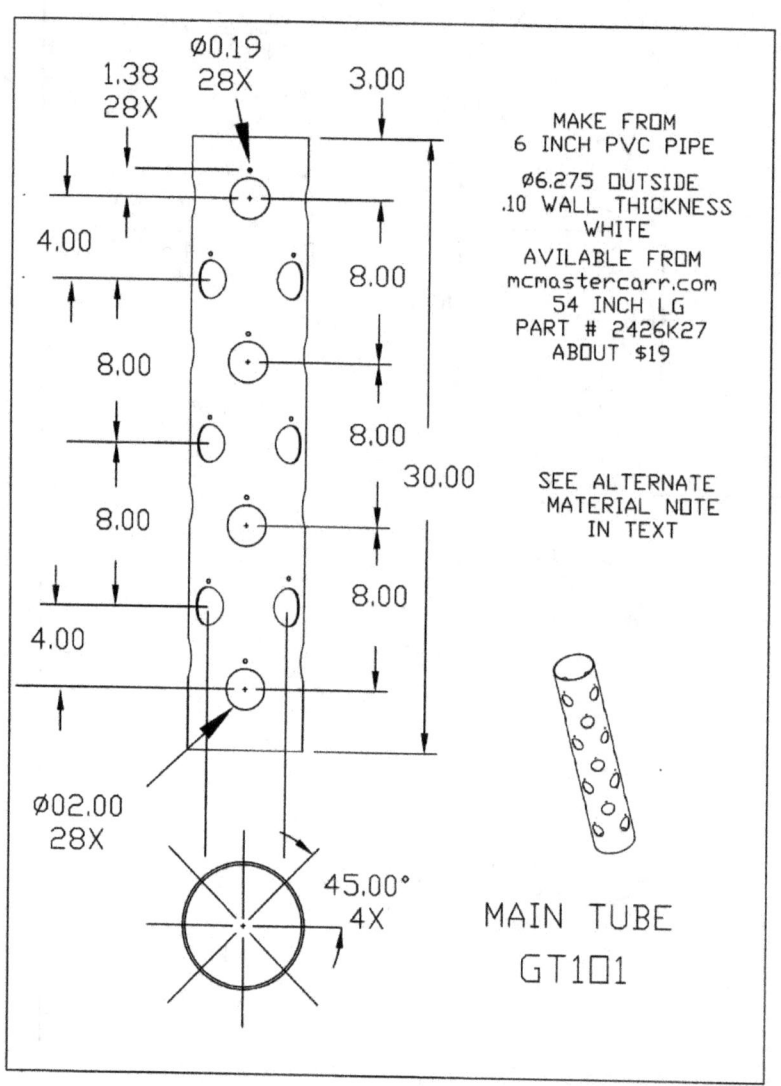

Main tube 4 foot tower

MAKE FROM 1 1/2 PVC
SCHEDULE 40 PIPE

AVAILABLE AT LOWES
OR HOME DEPOT

$5 FOR 5 FT

Ø.125
ONE WALL

Ø.25 2X
ONE WALL

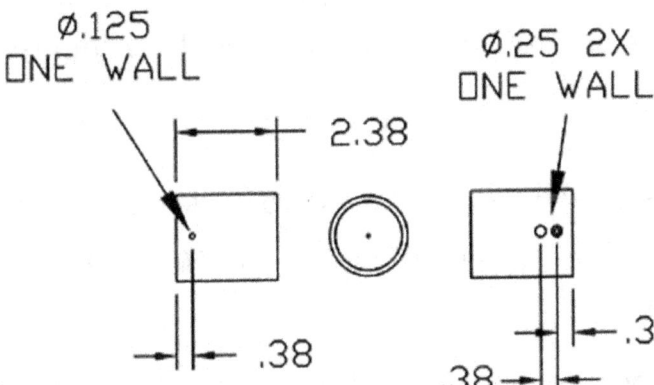

2.38

.38

.38

.38

Sugestion:
Drill .125 thru
both walls first

28 REQUIRED
FOR GT100
20 REQUIRED
FOR GTS100

GROW TUBE
GT105

Grow tube detail

The grow tubes GT105 are made from 1 1/2 inch schedule 40 PVC pipe cut in 2.3/8 inch lengths. Placed in the 2 inch diameter hole in the Main Tube, the sloppy fit allows the grow tubes to slant up enough for nutrient to drain back into the tube while soaking the plants roots.

A couple of Holes in the top side of the grow tube lets nutrient drizzle through the tube wetting the plant inside.

Making the grow tubes GT105 took a while but it is easy. Taking the 2 3/8 inch lengths and using a small pocket knife de bur the cuts.

Mark 3/8 inch from one end of each of the 20 or 28 pieces. With the tube clamped in a vise, drill a 1/8 inch hole through both walls of each tube.

If you have two drill motors. Use the second drill motor with a 1/4 inch drill to open up one wall of the 1/8 hole to 1/4 and then eyeball the location of the second 1/4 inch drain hole. The 1/4 inch hole locations are not critical since they are just for water to drizzle through.

This was easy once I figured it out. Go back and re-drill the 3/16 screw holes in the 6 inch tube slanting the hole towards the 2 inch hole making it easy to find the mating hole in the grow tube with the pointed end of the self-threading sheet metal stainless steel screw.

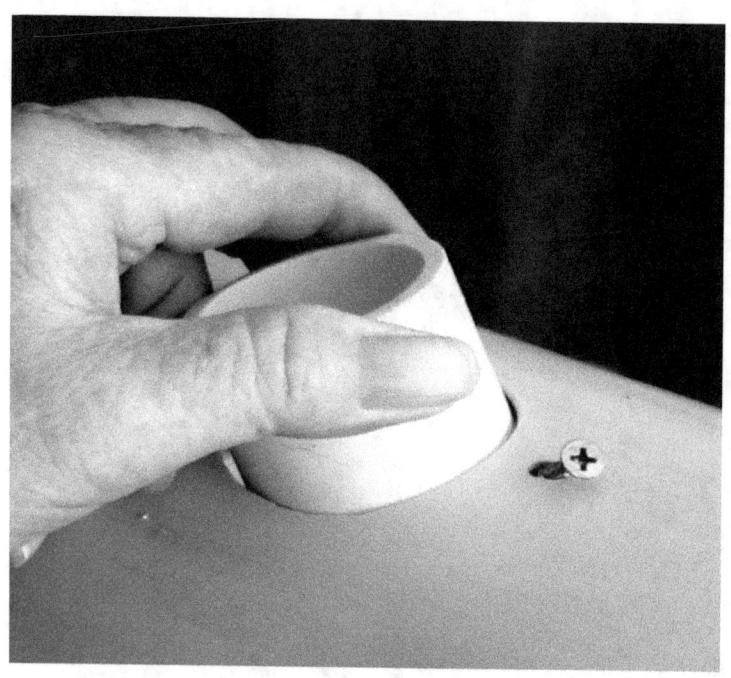

Tighten the screw almost to stripping.

The screw extends way into the grow tube providing a stop for planting seedlings and a spot for roots to grow around.

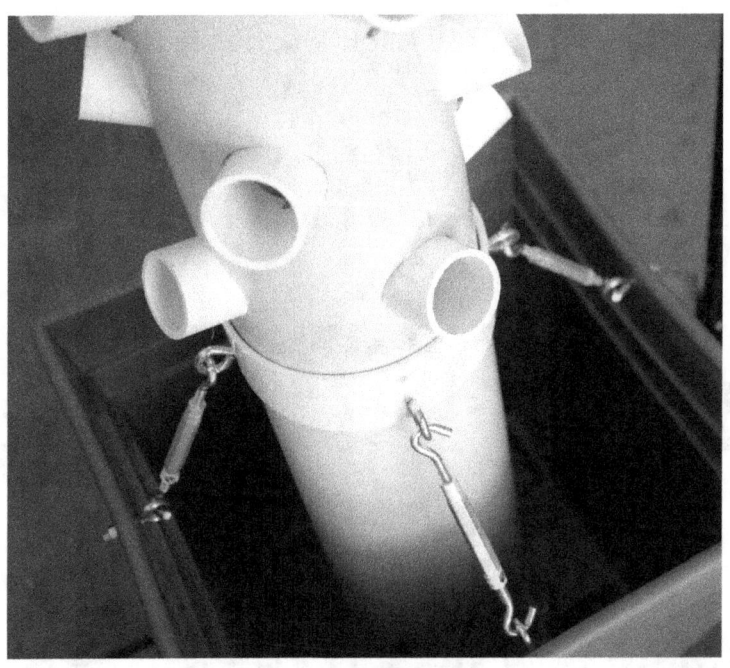

The lower support bolted to the lower coupling using the 4 eyebolts with nuts inside. With the main tube in place, drill a 1/8 hole for self-tapping screws into the main tube. This picture shows a molded square basin. I found them susceptible to cracking and leaking. Go for the resin basin. A few dollars more but much better

This is the upper coupling GT104. It is a tight slip fit onto the top of the main tube.

The ridge inside supports the water spreader and the fountain tube on the final assembly

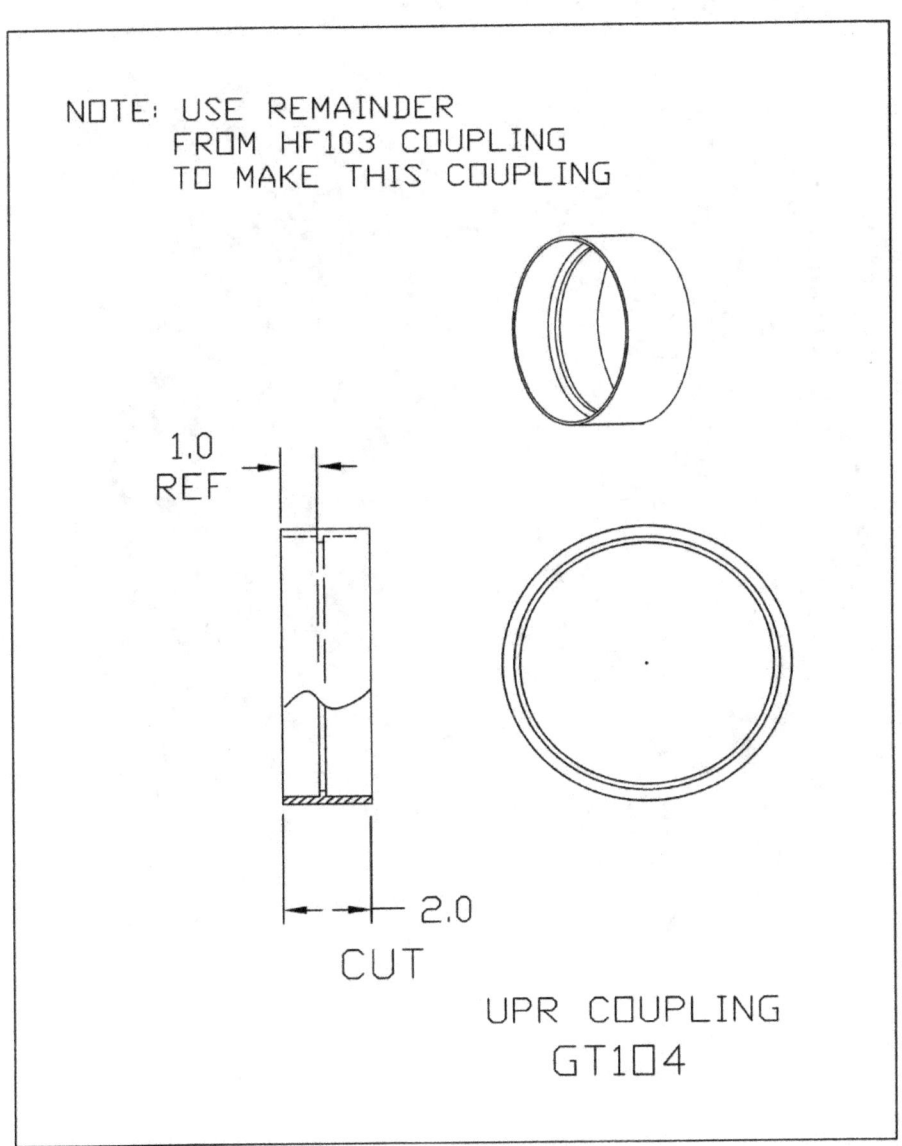

NOTE: USE REMAINDER
FROM HF103 COUPLING
TO MAKE THIS COUPLING

1.0
REF

2.0

CUT

UPR COUPLING
GT104

55

The green water spreader GT106 installs this side down in the upper coupling at final assembly.

MAKE FROM 6 INCH VALVE BOX LID

AVAILABLE AT LOWES $1.40

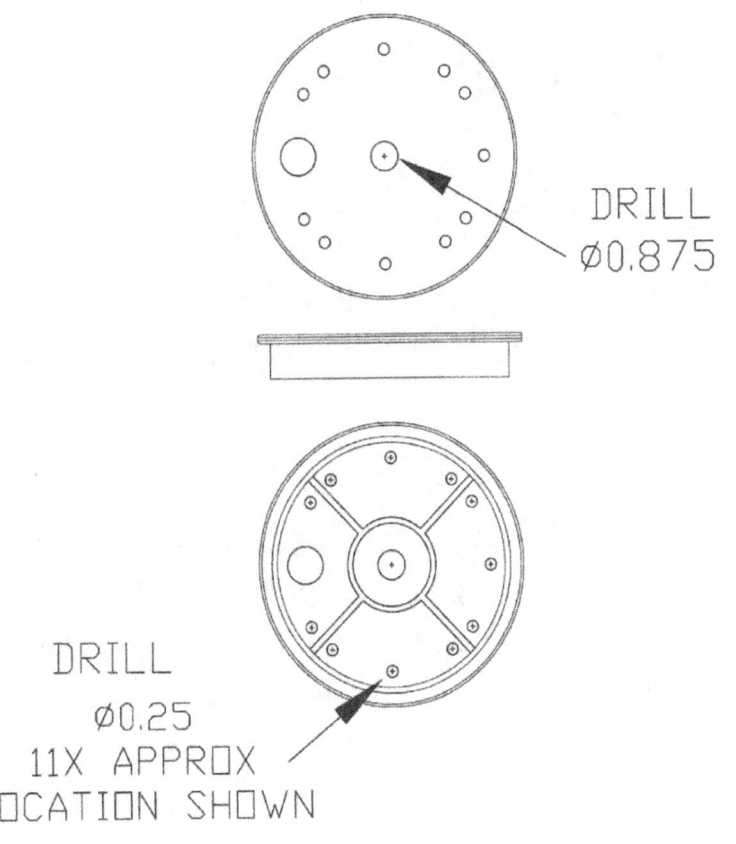

DRILL
Ø0.875

DRILL
Ø0.25
11X APPROX
LOCATION SHOWN

WATER SPREADER
GT106

Chapter 7

Final assembly

Take the completed base assembly and place the pump inside the support tube with the wire leading out through the large slot and into the slot in the rim of the basin.

Cut a 48 inch long piece of 1/2 inch PVC schedule 40 white pipe GT107. Couple this fountain pipe to the pump 1/2 inch outlet. Couple using a 6 inch length of 1/2 inch plastic hose pushed onto the pump fitting. You can now slide the 1/2 Inch PVC pipe over the hose as far as it will go. Do this before the main tube is installed on the base. Set the flow control on the end of the ECO370 pump to minimum. This will be about right for the 4 foot tower with a ECO 370 pump.

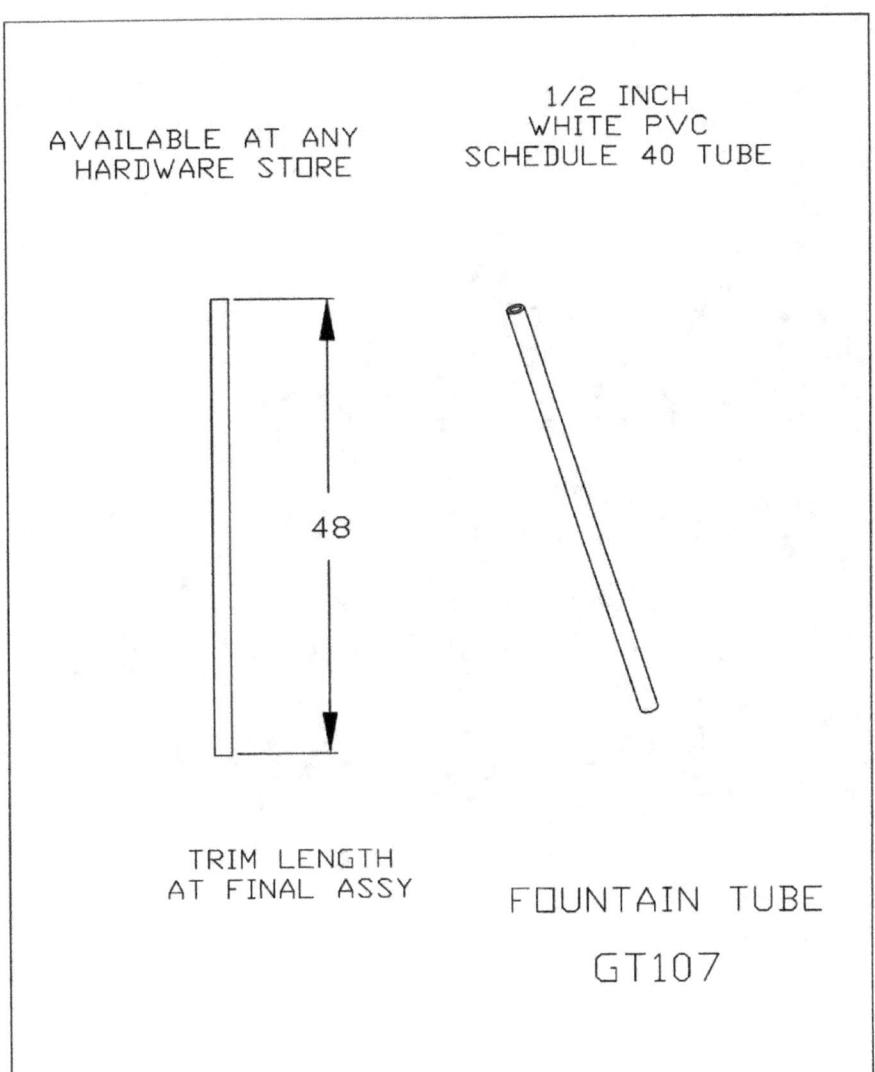

AVAILABLE AT ANY
HARDWARE STORE

1/2 INCH
WHITE PVC
SCHEDULE 40 TUBE

48

TRIM LENGTH
AT FINAL ASSY

FOUNTAIN TUBE

GT107

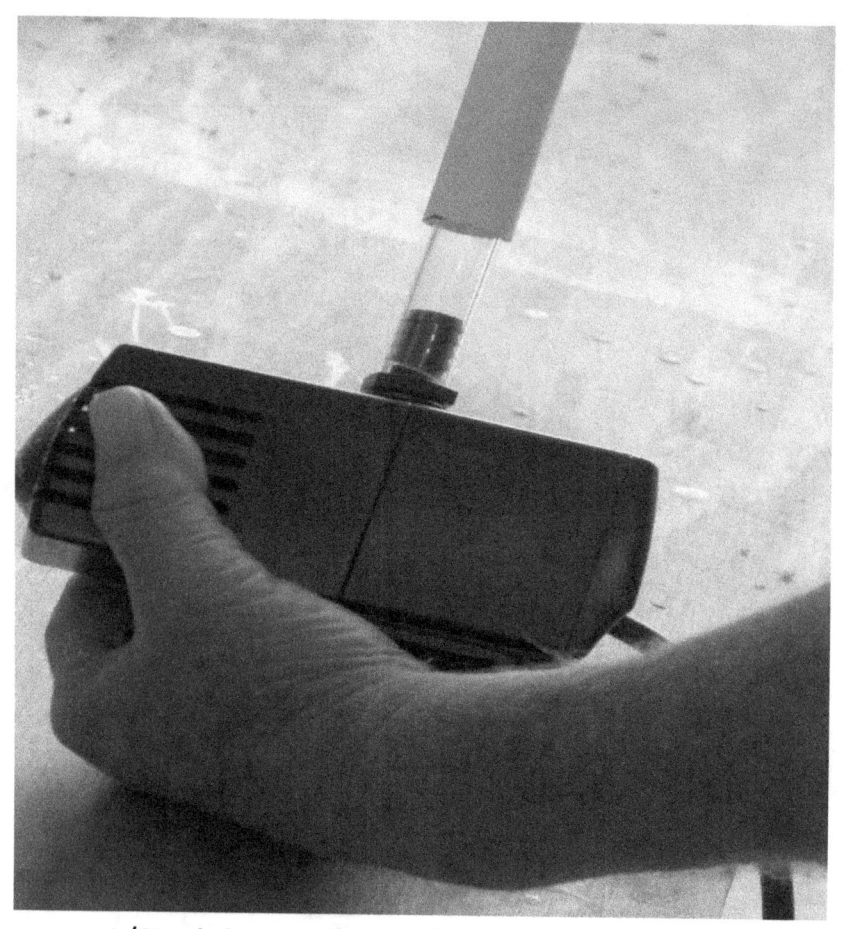

1/2inch hose 4 inches long on pump fitting.

Slide white 1/2 inch pvc pipe 48 inches long over the hose.

The Main Tube with grow tubes mounted is now is lifted over the fountain pipe and nested down into the base assembly plugging into the support tube lower coupling GT103. The main tube assembly is held erect by drilling a small hole through the lower coupling into the main tube and installing four #8 self- threading screws. Mark the relation of the main tube to the coupler with a felt pen for later ease of assembly.

The fountain tube is now poking out above the upper coupling GT104 that has previously been pressed onto the main tube.

Insert the water spreader GT106 over the fountain pipe and into the upper coupling GT104.

The fountain tube should now be protruding out through the green water spreader.

Trim the PVC fountain pipe about 1 inch above the water spreader.

You are now ready to plant your grow tower. Place your tower in a place where you can dump the water in case something goes wrong.

Fill the basin to the eye bolts with water and plug in the pump. Water will gurgle out of the fountain pipe and drain through the green water spreader.

If more water is desired turn dial on the end of pump to the right. If less is desired you can buy a smaller pump or try drilling some small holes in the fountain tube below the water spreader.

Assembly of the 3 foot tower is just the same except the pump, a ECO185 is smaller and does not have a flow adjustment.

Chapter 8

3 foot tower parts list

PARTS AND MATERIAL YOU NEED
TO BUILD A 3 FOOT HYDROPONIC TOWER

AVIABLE AT MOST HARDWARE STORES

PVC CLEAR CEMENT	$4 SMALL CAN
7 INCH AL ALLOY TURNBUCKEL 4 REQUIRED	$2 EA
1/4-20 EYE BOLT 4 REQUIRED	$1 EA
#10 X3/4 LG SH METAL SCREW 4 REQUIRED	$1 PACK
#6 X 1 1/4 INCH LG SH METAL SCREW Mc master Carr 90198A182	$7 50ea
1/2 INCH PVC PIPE 1 REQD PART Schedule 40 white 48 INCHES LONG	

PURCHASE PARTS

PUMP	1 REQD	ECO185 $12 greentrees.com
TIMER	1 REQD	Tork 601A $12 Walmart

MATERIAL REQUIRED

6 INCH PVC PIPE 24 INCHES LONG	2 REQD	lowes $18 each green
6 INCH PVC HUB X HUB COUPLING	1 REQD	HOMEDEPOT.COM $7.0 Mc Master Carr
6 INCH GREEN VALVE BOX LID	1 REQD	LOWES $1.40
PLASTIC BASIN 14 INCH DIA BY 13 INCH TALL		LOWES $16-$20

4 foot tower parts list

PARTS AND MATERIAL YOU NEED TO BUILD A 4 FOOT HYDROPONIC TOWER

AVIABLE AT MOST HARDWARE STORES

PVC CLEAR CEMENT $4 SMALL CAN

7 INCH AL ALLOY TURNBUCKEL $2 EA
    4 REQUIRED

1/4-20 EYE BOLT $1 EA
    8 REQUIRED

#10 X3/4 LG SH METAL SCREW $1 PACK
    4 REQUIRED

#6 X 1 1/4 INCH LG SH METAL SCREW $7 50ea
    Mc master Carr 90198A182

1/2 INCH PVC PIPE
48 INCHES LONG   1 REQD   PART Schedule 40 white

PURCHASE PARTS

PUMP   1 REQD   ECO370 $12
    greentrees.com

TIMER   1 REQD   Tork 601A $12
    Walmart

MATERIAL REQUIRED

6 INCH PVC PIPE   Mc Master Carr
54 INCHES LONG   1 REQD   Part # 2426K27

6 INCH PVC HUB X HUB   HOMEDEPOT.COM $7.0
    COUPLING   1 REQD   Mc Master Carr

6 INCH GREEN   LOWES $1.40
VALVE BOX LID   1 REQD

PLASTIC BASIN 14 INCH DIA   LOWES
BY 13 INCH TALL $16-$20

Chapter 9

Planting your tower

It's pretty easy and fun to do and will be very satisfying when you fill the basin with water.

Move your tower into the sun. Let the pump run for several hours allowing the chlorine in the water evaporate.

Add nutrient, plant seedlings and set the timer for fifteen minutes on and fifteen minutes off.

Watch your seedlings grow.

Enjoy your crop of fresh vegetables.

I bought nutrient from www.GardenTowers.com. It was probably a major factor in my success.

There are lots of suppliers of nutrient to experiment with including mixing your own. This is probably a risky undertaking unless you are a botanist.

You can purchase molded square foam growing blocks that are a nice snug fit in the 1 1/2 tube. It is very cheap and available at most nurseries or any hydroponic supply store. See figure page 66.

The advantage of using the foam blocks is not only to grow from seed and to hold the plant in place but also to saturate the area with water providing fluid in case of a power failure or shut down of your pump for an hour or so.

Good luck.

Planted from seed and then transplanted to the tower while in the foam jacket

Rosemary

Strawberry

Oregano

Tomato is about to have blossoms

Chapter 10

Tower care and maintenance

First off never let the pump run dry. It will wreck it in a hurry.

Keep the timer out of the rain and away from sprinklers.

With the basin full of water add about a 1/4 cup of tonic A and a 1/4 cup of tonic B from Tower Garden.com The large basin is about 8 gallons and the smaller about 6 gallons.

Add measured portion of nutrient when refilling the basin. Check at least once a week or more often in hot weather.

You should be able to run the unit for a whole season without taking anything apart including the pump. The pump has a pretty good filter keeping dirt and junk out.

If the pump does get clogged you can lift off the main tube with all the plants undisturbed by removing the 4 self-tapping screws and lifting the main tube off. You can reach into the support tube and lift out the pump. Snap off the cover and clean the impeller and filter system. This should not take over a half hour; then you can replace the clean pump and get the system running again.

When placing the main tube with growing plants be sure to stuff hanging roots back inside the lower support.

When winter comes if you are in a cold climate be sure to at least drain all the water before a freeze sets in. A freeze will crack your pump open and maybe even split the basin in two.

There's no reason why your system will not last for years if cared for. The pumps specified are the best and have only one moving part. It can be replaced if needed for a few bucks.

Chapter 11

General information and reminders.

Run a fresh filling of water a couple hours

before planting to let the chlorine evaporate.

Wash out the roots of seedlings to about

90%. Let the remaining dirt settle in the

basin before running the pump. This small amount of dirt

won't matter.

Suppliers

Lowes has almost everything you need to

build a Hydroponic Fun Tower. Some

Lowes do not carry the 6 inch fittings.

Home depot has on the internet the 6

inch thin and thick wall sewer pipe.

Order and pick up at your local store to save

Shipping cost.

I found Groves in Boise has a complete

supply at the lowest prices. They may be

in your town also.

Greentrees in Santa Clarita Ca. has a

complete line of pumps, timers and

hydroponic supplies online.

www.Greentrees.com

Tower garden has an excellent

supply of Hydroponic supplies. That's

where my nutrient comes from

www.towergarden.com

www.McMasterCarr.com Has just about everything you can think of in stock with immediate delivery. A great resource for all your projects. Maybe not the cheapest and shipping is always a consideration.

Chapter 12

Thanks for buying this book. I hope you will build or buy a tower. See www.hydroponicfun.com to buy a complete ready to plant tower.

Plant your tower with the magic of living things. And enjoy a bite or two from your tower garden

Whatever path you take I know you

will enjoy hydroponics and have fun with the results.

Please send me pictures of your tower

however it comes out and certainly feel free

to redesign to fit your needs.

You might build a bunch and sell them at your

local farmers market and make a few dollars.

I can be reached at   sandls@cableone.net

or at hydroponicfun@gmail.com

www.ingramcontent.com/pod-product-compliance
Lightning Source LLC
Chambersburg PA
CBHW070808290526
45795CB00002B/658